PILOTS ON FOOD STAMPS

An Inside Look At Why Your Flight Was Cancelled

Ben Mandell

PILOTS ON FOOD STAMPS
Copyright © 2014 by Amazing Publishing, Inc.

All rights reserved. No part of this book may be reproduced or transmitted in any form or by any means without written permission from the author.

ISBN 978-0692266304

Printed in USA

Dedication

This book is dedicated to the professional current and future airline pilots who transport millions of people safely and efficiently across the United States every month.

Table of Contents

Foreword 7
Preface 9
Introduction 11
The Planes Had To Be Parked 13
Your Pilot Is A Trained Professional 15
Twenty Eight Dollars And Eight Cents 19
Shall We Stay Or Shall We Go? 23
Endeavor Air 31
Upgrading To The Majors 37
How Pilots Are Paid 43
Pilots Are A Dime A Dozen 47
How The Industry Jumped The Shark 53
Airline Executives In Denial 59
Mainline, We Have A Problem 65
The Sky Is Not Looking Good Out West 71
Where Is All This Going? 77
Why Airline Executives Do The Things 83
Upgrade Times And Pay 91
There Is Only One Solution 95

Foreword

"Incredible!" you might say, "Pilots qualifying for food stamps. Surely you must be joking!"

We see airline Pilots in their pressed suits and crisp shirts as they walk through the airport terminals, hear their calm, friendly voices informing passengers of flight time and weather conditions on the plane and assume they are making six figure salaries, or somewhere close to that.

Wrong, wrong, wrong!

This book is a true to life account of the current pilot crisis facing the nation; its origin, the current status and what needs to be done to fix this problem.

If your Physician put in six to eight years of medical education, training and internship in order to provide you with the best, up to date medical care, would you expect him or her to be paid less than that of a fast food worker with much less training?

Would it be fair if the Physician's salary was calculated only on the actual time he or she was in the office or in surgery with the patient, without taking into consideration the doctor's time spent on patient telephone calls, availability for the times on standby when the doctor was "on call", travel to and from the clinic, hospital or office as well as supervisory and administrative duties? Why should a pilot only get paid for his or her actual flight time?

Is it fair for airline passengers to have their flights cancelled and planes grounded because there are not enough qualified pilots?

As we read this book we must ask ourselves if we will garner the political will to demand better wages for our pilots and if we will hold our elected officials accountable for ensuring adequate airline and passenger safety. And then we must act to make sure the job gets done.

A Must Read!

Preface

Poverty wages are the reason we currently face a pilot shortage in the United States.

In January 2014, airlines publically announced for the first time that they were cancelling flights because of a lack of qualified pilots.

The lack of pilots had been building for several years, but in 2014, the industry simply ran out of enough qualified pilot applicants. The planes had to be parked and flights had to be cancelled.

If you have not yet been affected by a flight cancellation, there is a 35 percent chance that you will be in the near future. If your flight is cancelled, this book will help you understand why.

Introduction

In the United States there are about 30,000 airline flights per day. It is a pretty remarkable system that safely transports more than 1.5 million passengers daily.

Each of those 30,000 airline flights must have at least two qualified and trained pilots in order for the aircraft to get off of the ground and land safely at the destination with sometimes hundreds of passengers aboard.

In 2014, becoming a commercial airline pilot requires an Airline Transport Pilot (ATP) rating which also includes specific training milestones as dictated by FAA rules and regulations. An ATP rating generally requires a minimum of 1500 flight hours although there are some restricted ATP ratings available at 1000 and 1200 hours under certain conditions. Keep in mind this is the *minimum* number of hours. Often it will take more than the minimum to get to the airlines.

Today, if a person desires to have a career as a commercial airline pilot; the cost of training to be employable as a first officer at a commercial airline can exceed $250,000 and take six and a half to eight years by the time all is said and done.

Yet, the airlines insist on paying professional highly trained and skilled pilot first officers less than the janitor at the local fast food restaurant. This has resulted in pilots being paid poverty wages. Pilots actually do qualify for food stamps.

In the past, no one really cared because it did not affect anyone but the pilots. If you think about it, the airlines sort of keep the pilots in hiding and out of sight. You generally will not see pilots on television or doing interviews. The information in this book is just not known by the general public.

Now that flights are being cancelled, a lot of paying passengers will be affected by these cancelled flights.

Chapter One
The Planes Had To Be Parked

Training to become a commercial airline pilot is expensive. In 2014, it can cost $250,000 by the time all of the training and ratings are completed.

It will take six to eight years, for a pilot, to accomplish this training and gather the required number of hours to be eligible to be employed by a commercial airline as a first officer.

A first officer is also known as a co-pilot. As a general rule a pilot is hired as a first officer, flying in the right seat and will move up to captain and fly in the left seat as he/she gains experience and seniority at the airline.

There is a lot of misinformation out there about how much pilots make. The industry has kept the numbers confusing for decades because it benefits them to do so.

In effect, what has been happening is that the airlines have not been paying a living wage to many of their pilots. The new hire pilots have been subsidizing the training costs for multi-million and multi-billion dollar airlines while having to live on poverty wages for many years.

You might think this will not affect you. You might think that this does not matter. You might think that if the pilots do not like the poverty wages, then they should go and find something else to do where they can make a living wage.

A lot of pilots have left the industry and they have gone on to careers that pay better. It is not that these pilots wanted to leave; it was simply economics. How do you (as a trained professional) tell a spouse that you are going to be on food stamps for the next six years?

According to a February 2014, Government Accountability Office study, 7,858 US citizen ATP rated pilots are flying overseas for foreign carriers. The reason: foreign carriers pay more.

Poverty wages are the reason we currently face a pilot shortage in the United States.

In February 2014, airlines announced for the first time that they were cancelling flights because of a lack of qualified pilots.

The lack of pilots had been building for several years, but in 2014, the industry simply ran out of qualified pilot applicants.

And the planes had to be parked.

Chapter Two
Your Pilot Is a Trained Professional

Poverty wages are the reason that we now face a pilot shortage in the United States.

A career as a professional airline pilot requires professional training. While a college degree is not an absolute requirement, many pilots do obtain their training and college degree at the same university. To qualify for an ATP rating with a reduced number of hours, you must obtain *all* of your training at one of the approved universities that offers a degree along with the flight training.

Pilot training is difficult and has a high washout rate. More than two-thirds of the students who begin their pilot training do not obtain a pilot license. They simply quit. So it is a real accomplishment for someone to complete their commercial pilot training and ratings.

There are many facilities for a pilot to obtain training. Some are simple flight schools. Some are approved universities. All pilot licenses are issued by the Federal Aviation Administration (FAA) after a pilot has received his/her training.

Embry-Riddle Aeronautical University in Daytona Beach, Florida is a well-known approved pilot training university. The minimum estimated cost to attend Embry-Riddle to obtain a four-year degree along with commercial flight training is $207,080 in 2014. I will use Embry-Riddle as an example throughout this book. However, I need to make it clear that the career path and timeline that a student takes at Embry-Riddle is going to be much the same as any other aviation university training program.

The aviation universities, like Embry-Riddle, are not doing anything bad and I don't want to imply that they are. The pilot poverty wage problem and pilot shortage are not caused by the schools.

If a student does graduate from one of the aviation universities, like Embry-Riddle, he can be hired by the airlines with 1000 hours of flight time instead of the mandated 1500 flight hours. So there is a one to two year career advantage if a student does all of their training at one of the aviation universities simply because they can be hired by the airlines with 500 fewer flight hours.

When you finish your flight training at Embry Riddle, you will have between 190 and 250 flight hours. If you have your Certified Flight Instructor (CFI) rating you will then be able to earn money as a flight instructor. You still will not yet qualify to be hired by the airlines as a first officer. You will need to spend another two to four years building flight time as a flight instructor, towing banners or doing oil pipeline patrols. This will cost you time. You will not make much money, but your living costs (rent, utilities, insurance, gas, etc.) will continue on.

As you can see, even in the best of circumstances it will take you at least six years from the time you enter Embry-Riddle to get enough hours for an airline to hire you as a professional pilot.

If you are like most college students today, once you graduate from Embry-Riddle you might have more than $200,000 in student loan debt that has to be re-paid starting six months after you graduate or leave school. You will have a student loan payment of more than $1100.00 a month for 30 years.

You are entitled to a return on your investment. You should be paid as a professional. You have worked hard. You have completed a professional training program. Yet the airlines do not value your training as pilot.

Almost all new airline pilots start at the regional airlines. There are about seventeen still in business as I write this book. I expect there will be fewer as time goes on. The reason for this is because the regional airlines are not going to be able to hire enough pilots to fly their aircraft.

The regional airlines fly about half of the commercial airline flights each day in the United States. The regional airlines feed passengers from smaller airports to larger airports. Most regional airlines have a major airlines name painted on the side of the aircraft. The idea is to give the passenger a seamless travel experience on what appears to be one airline.

After a pilot has completed $250,000 in training and dedicated six to eight years of his life, he can apply to a regional airline, such as Endeavor Air. Endeavor Air is owned by Delta

Air Lines and all Endeavor flights carry Delta passengers. The Endeavor aircraft are painted to look like the other Delta aircraft. The Endeavor aircraft have the Delta logo on them. Somewhere near the door (in small letters) there will be a sticker that says Operated by Endeavor Air.

At Endeavor Air a pilot will be paid $22,500 the first year and $29,700 the second year. During the third year the pilot will be paid $31,500. A pilot will likely spend nine years at Endeavor Air with hopes of one day flying the larger planes for the mainline carriers. During these nine years, the pilot will make less than $35,500 a year for most of the years employed. The pilot will not get a pay raise until he can move up to captain and that will take at least seven years.

Meanwhile those $1,100 a month student loan payments are going on each and every month for 30 years. It has been eight to 11 years since the pilot first walked into Embry-Riddle and he is now making less than $35,500 a year. The assistant manager at Taco Bell makes more than he does and he does not have $200,000 in student loan debt.

Chapter Three
Twenty Eight Dollars And Eight Cents

Colgan Flight 3407 crashed into a house near the Buffalo, New York airport on Feb. 12, 2009. All 49 people on board and one person in the house were killed.

If you were one of the unfortunate folks who had boarded flight 3407 in Newark, New Jersey, you would have thought you were on a Continental Airlines flight. The outside of the plane was painted in the Continental colors and the Continental logo was on the tail. The aircraft said Continental Connection in big letters on the fuselage. The seatback pockets contained the Continental Airlines magazine. (Continental Airlines later merged with United Airlines and that same Continental logo is now on all of the new United Airlines aircraft tails.)

Somewhere near the door, on the outside of the plane, it said, in much smaller letters, "Operated by Colgan Air."

So why would a major airline such as Continental go to all of the trouble to make the Colgan Air plane look and act like a Continental plane?

The answer is something called a codeshare and money. A codeshare is when one airline sells the ticket on more than one carrier and makes it appear like it is all one airline. It is designed to be a seamless travel experience for the passenger.

So why do airlines such as Continental even have codeshares?

The reason major airlines have codeshares with the regional airlines in the United States is because they can get away with it.

It is cheaper for a major airline to outsource its flying to the regional airlines. The regionals spend less on aircraft and they spend less on pilots.

Airlines often make the excuse and will try to blame the passengers by saying that the passengers are demanding cheaper airline tickets and that is the reason for the regionals.

Major airlines (American, Delta, United and USAir) are set up on a hub and spoke system in the US.

For example Delta Air Lines currently operates hubs in Atlanta, Detroit, Minneapolis, New York City and Salt Lake City. Hundreds of flights a day fly in and out of an airline hub.

There are two kinds of passenger traffic in a hub city. There is connecting feed traffic and there is originating traffic.

Originating traffic is when a passenger first boards a plane in a hub city. Connecting feed traffic is when a passenger first boards a plane in another city and flies through and connects within a hub to fly to another city.

As a general rule, less than 40 percent of passengers actually originate in a hub city. The other passenger feed is from the connecting traffic.

Regional airlines account for over 50 percent of the airline flights each day. These regional airlines feed connecting passengers to the major airlines.

Major airlines would love to get rid of regional airlines. They keep them around because they feed more than 35 percent of the passengers to the major airlines. If the major airlines did not have these connecting feed passengers, they would become unprofitable as a going concern.

Flight 3407 was operated by Colgan Air for Continental Airlines. There were at least two pilots on board this aircraft as required by FAA regulations.

There is a saying in the industry that in air crashes, the pilots always get the blame. It would be no different for flight 3407. So I will not get into a discussion about this.

Flight 3407 would have taken about one hour and five minutes to fly from Newark to Buffalo. It is a distance of about 300 air miles.

The first officer was Rebecca Shaw and the captain was Marvin Renslow.

There were 44 passengers in the back of the plane and there were two flight attendants.

I went to a seminar about a year after this crash and there was a representative from one of the insurance companies there. I spent a few minutes speaking with him. It turned out this was a very expensive plane crash for the insurance companies. The insurance companies paid out much more than they had expected.

His biggest surprise was how little the pilots made. He went on to say that the pilots were fatigued and that a $50 hotel room may have prevented the crash.

First Officer Rebecca Shaw was paid $28.08 to fly the plane with 44 passengers from Newark to Buffalo. That is about 64 cents a passenger. Not enough to pay for a hotel room.

Chapter Four
Shall We Stay Or Shall We Go?

I have pointed out that the major airlines would love to get rid of the regional airlines if they could. In fact American and Delta have tried to shed their wholly owned regional airlines.

Delta actually owned four different regional airlines from the years 1999-2012 and got rid of them all.

Delta sold ASA Airlines on Sept. 5, 2005

Delta sold Compass Airlines in July 2010.

Delta sold Mesaba Airlines on July 1, 2010, to Pinnacle Airlines Corp.

Delta purchased Comair Airlines in 1999 and actually shut it down on Sept. 29, 2012. It seems no one wanted to buy it. At that point Delta was out of the business of owning regional airlines. (That would quickly change)

American Airlines has attempted to find a buyer for wholly owned American Eagle Airlines, for at least the past six years and no one has been interested. American has now changed the name of American Eagle to Envoy Air and still operates the airline because it *must* have the passenger feed.

Most of the regional airlines (the ones without their real name on the side of the fuselage) use the same business model.

The major airlines put out bids for certain routes and the regionals basically beat each other up by offering the lowest bid to transport passengers from Point A to Point B. It is a race to the bottom.

In the past, the majors have played one regional airline against another, all in an effort to convince them to fly passengers cheaply from Point A to Point B in order to capture their business.

In the early 1990's, the 50-seat regional jet was developed. Up to this point, the regionals did not fly jets. They flew only propeller aircraft. At that time, the majors did not fly anything smaller than an 80-seat DC-9 or Fokker jet.

Because mainline pilots do not downgrade to smaller aircraft, this meant that the only place the 50-seat regional jets would fit in would be at the regional airlines. This also presented a problem for the industry.

Regional airlines and mainline airlines were divided by the type of aircraft they flew. Mainline airlines flew only jets. Regional airlines flew only propeller planes. It was pretty easy to tell them apart.

Most mainline pilots were represented by unions and had union contracts. The airline industry is so big that union contracts are pretty much a necessity. Those mainline pilot contracts often prohibited the regional airlines from flying jet aircraft.

Mainline airlines went back to the negotiating table, with the unions, to get permission for the regional partners to operate the regional jets. There was some give and take as there is in all negotiations. The end result was that the majority of mainline pilots agreed to allow the regional airlines to fly jets provided those jets did not exceed 50 seats.

The intent was that the regional airlines would not take the routes away from mainline planes that were being flown at that time. The regional jet was sold as an aircraft to fly point to point. There was never anything mentioned about flying regional jets between large population areas. They were intended for point to point service usually bypassing a hub.

In the beginning, it pretty much worked out that way. But in the late 1990's there was an exemption that the regional airlines had carved out that would change the course of aviation history in the US. The exemption is known as the Wendell H Ford Aviation Investment And Reform Act for the 21St Century.

Airline routes in the US were deregulated in 1978. Up to that time, certain specific airlines were assigned to certain specific point to point city routes. Another airline could not fly on a route that was already being serviced by an existing airline. For example, if you were going to fly from Los Angeles to Atlanta, that route would only be flown by Delta or Eastern Airlines. No other airline could fly that route.

When the regional aircraft were developed in the early 1990's, airline routes were already deregulated, and any domestic airline could fly almost anywhere within the United States.

The key word is almost. There were some airports in major population areas (Boston, Chicago, Los Angeles, New York and Washington, DC) that were slot controlled.

What this meant was that other airlines generally could not add any routes to, or from, those cities because the airspace was considered full. There were not any takeoff or landing slots available. There are only so many minutes in an hour. A runway can handle a maximum of 20 takeoffs and landings an hour under ideal conditions.

At some point in the late 1990's the regional jet lobby was able to convince Congress to exempt regional jets from any slot requirements, to New York City airports, under the Wendell H Ford Aviation Act. This made absolutely no sense, but somehow they were able to get this provision passed.

What this did was create a land rush for regional jets at airports in the New York City area. Airlines started flying regional jets from almost any city, previously unserved within 1000 miles into New York's LaGuardia and JFK airports.

This opened up a new business model for the regional airlines. They could transport passengers on 50-seat jet aircraft. They could gain more slots to and from the most populated and most profitable city in the United States.

In the early 1990's the majors had already started taking routes away from their higher paid mainline pilots and transferring those routes to the regionals.

With the Wendell H Ford Aviation Act, the regional airlines grew and grew. The regional airlines made a lot of money in the late 1990s and early 2000s. Some of them built up a lot of cash and when Sept. 11th 2001 came, those regional airlines were in the right place at the right time.

In 2005, US Airways needed $250 million to emerge from its first bankruptcy. US Airways was able to obtain half of that money ($125 million) from a regional airline, Air Wisconsin in the form of a loan. Without Air Wisconsin, USAir may not have been able to emerge from bankruptcy and may have gone out of business. Fortunately things worked out and USAir eventually merged with American Airlines to become the world's largest airline.

PINNACLE AIRLINES

This chapter would not be complete without discussing Pinnacle Airlines. Pinnacle Airlines was founded in 1985 and grew to become one of the largest regional airlines in the US. In 2007 Pinnacle was flying high and making a lot of money. On Jan. 18, 2007, Pinnacle purchased Colgan Air and continued to operate it as an independent airline. (Colgan was the operator of Flight 3407, which crashed in Buffalo)

On July 1, 2010, Pinnacle purchased Mesaba Airlines. Mesaba Airlines had been in operation since 1944. At the end of 2010, Pinnacle operated three airlines, Pinnacle, Colgan and

Mesaba. Pinnacle flew flights for Continental, Delta, United, and US Airways.

The recession started hitting Pinnacle (and the other airlines) during the second quarter of 2008. Airlines began to lose money. Fuel prices were up to levels never seen before.

In early 2008 Pinnacle stopped hiring pilots. Pinnacle would not attempt to hire pilots again until 2011 believing it had enough pilots to keep its aircraft flying. In the meantime, the pilot recruiting department was dismantled.

In late 2010, Pinnacle started cancelling hundreds of flights each month because there were not enough pilots to fly its aircraft. This was not public knowledge.

In 2011, Pinnacle notified Continental and United that it was cancelling their contracts in an effort to get things under control. Pinnacle moved many Mesaba pilots over to Pinnacle to fill the empty seats. That left Pinnacle only flying for Delta.

Delta was not happy with the flights being cancelled and stranding their passengers. There were meetings with the Pinnacle executives.

The straw that broke the camel's back came in February 2011 when Pinnacle cancelled hundreds of flights to and from the Memphis hub because of a lack of flight crews. This stranded thousands of Delta passengers and disrupted the Delta system. Delta sent a letter to the Pinnacle CEO indicating that flights would be cancelled if the problem was not immediately fixed.

Without notice, on March 15, 2011, Phillip Trenary, the longtime, president and CEO of Pinnacle, suddenly stepped down and left the company. This was an indicator of things to come.

On March 23, 2011, Delta Air Lines notified Pinnacle that it was cancelling 25 percent of Pinnacle's daily flights out of the Memphis hub. Delta really had no choice, because Pinnacle had not hired enough pilots to fly the growing schedules. In effect, Delta, "right sized" Pinnacle based on the number of pilots at the airline.

When you no longer have 25 percent of your income, you start to lose money and bleed red ink. That is exactly what happened with Pinnacle.

On Jan. 4, 2012, Mesaba Airlines ceased operations. Mesaba was one of the world's safest air carriers and recorded no fatalities during its 68 years in business.

On April 1, 2012 Pinnacle Airlines and its subsidiaries filed for protection under Chapter 11 of the United States Bankruptcy Code. Pinnacle shut down Colgan Air while in bankruptcy.

In the normal course of regional airline life, Pinnacle would have been shut down and liquidated. It was losing money and only had one customer which was Delta Air Lines.

Delta was no longer in the regional airline business, but even though Delta had been part of the cause that resulted in Pinnacle going into bankruptcy, (because Delta cancelled 25 percent of its flights, and income) Delta still needed Pinnacle because it could not find another regional airline to fly those routes.

Delta funded Pinnacle while they were in bankruptcy because it had to have the passenger feed.

Pinnacle Airlines emerged from Chapter 11 bankruptcy on May 1, 2013, as a wholly owned subsidiary of Delta Air Lines. This was not because Delta wanted to be back in the regional airline business. It was because Delta must have the passenger feed that Pinnacle provides.

On August 1, 2013, Delta changed the name of Pinnacle Airlines to Endeavor Air.

Chapter Five
Endeavor Air

Endeavor Air is one of the 17 regional airlines currently operating in the United States.

Endeavor Air is 100 percent owned by Delta Air Lines and it flies 100 percent of its flights for Delta Air Lines. All Endeavor Air passengers are Delta passengers.

Endeavor Air has 150 aircraft and all of them say "Delta" on the side of the fuselage. These aircraft fly more than 850 flights per day to more than 100 cities in the US and Canada. Every passenger on every Endeavor flight is a Delta passenger.

Delta handles all ticketing for all passengers who fly on Endeavor. You cannot purchase a ticket from Endeavor Air. You must purchase a ticket from Delta or a travel agent that issues Delta tickets.

This is an important distinction, because airline executives like to shuffle things around and make things appear to be different than they really are.

So to review, Endeavor is 100 percent owned by Delta. Endeavor flies only Delta passengers. The Endeavor planes have

Delta graphics on them. You can only purchase a ticket on an Endeavor flight through Delta.

All income provided to Endeavor is from Delta Air Lines. Delta decides how much it is going to pay Endeavor Airlines. Delta decides who is going to sit on the board of directors of Endeavor Airlines.

In effect, Delta controls Endeavor Airlines. What Delta wants—Delta gets as far as Endeavor Airlines is concerned.

Delta Air Lines made a profit of $10.5 billion in 2013. This is the most money that any airline has ever made in the history of the world.

This multi-billion-dollar corporation (Delta) currently pay the new pilots, which they cause to be hired at Endeavor, a gross total of $22,000 a year.

These would be the same pilots who spent over $200,000 to get the proper training and certifications necessary to become an airline pilot.

Delta will tell you that their pilots actually make more than $22,000 a year. And there is some truth to that for those who have been there for many years, but it is going to be many years before anyone gets to a living wage as a pilot at Delta's wholly owned Endeavor Air.

Delta will tell you that Endeavor Air is a separate airline. And that also would also be true. The question that you should be asking is, "Why is Endeavor Air a separate airline?"

Why is Endeavor not merged with mainline Delta? After all the planes already have the Delta name painted on them. Delta already pays all of Endeavors expenses. Yet, Delta which has tried desperately to get rid of its regional airlines, holds onto this part of the regional airline business model.

Remember, all of Endeavors passengers are Delta passengers. All of Endeavors planes say Delta on the side of them. All of the Endeavor seatback pockets contain the Delta Sky magazine.

If you go to Delta's website and click on Aircraft, you will see pictures and details of all the aircraft that Delta has in its system. This includes all of the planes flown by Endeavor Airlines.

As an example, let us look at a typical new hire Delta pilot at Endeavor. Keep in mind that beginning commercial pilots cannot go directly to Delta mainline. Currently, beginning commercial pilots must go to a regional airline like Endeavor Air.

Earlier, I gave an example of an Embry-Riddle graduate who would go to work for Endeavor Air. Let's expand upon this further.

The new pilot will be 24 to 26 years old under the best case scenario. He will have spent more than $200,000 getting the required hours and training to be hired by a regional airline such as Endeavor Air. He will have spent four years in college and then another two to four years building his hours. He will have a student debt of more than $200,000 with monthly student loan payments of more than $1,100 a month for 30 years.

Endeavor will hire this new pilot and pay him $22,000 a year. That works out to $1,833 a month before taxes.

So let us take a look at how much the pilot is paid out of your ticket that Delta sold to you.

A new hire pilot will likely have to work weekends and holidays because schedules are based on the seniority system and most pilots would prefer to take weekends off. That leaves the weekend trips for the new hires. A new hire pilot will likely be assigned to fly the CRJ200 aircraft at Endeavor.

Let us say you purchase a ticket to fly on Delta from Dayton, Ohio to Detroit Michigan. Endeavor Air Flight 3632 flies on Friday afternoon and leaves at 5:30 p.m. Endeavor uses a CRJ-200 aircraft on this route. It is not a long flight and will take about 45 minutes if the weather cooperates. You will pay an average fare on this route of $283.99. This might be a route that a new hire pilot would fly.

Delta will pay the newly hired first officer (aka the co-pilot) $18.33 to fly this route.

On this 50-seat CRJ200 aircraft that works out to less than 37 cents a passenger that is being paid to the first officer pilot.

Next year, Delta will pay the first officer $24.75 to fly this flight.

If the first officer is there in year three, he will be paid $26.24 to fly this route.

At year four, the first officer tops out in first officer pay and he will be paid $27.74 to fly this flight from now on until he upgrades to captain.

At the current seniority list, it will take at least six years to upgrade to captain at Endeavor Air. At the point the first officer is promoted to captain he will be paid $50.99 to fly that route. This will be 13 years after the pilot first set foot into Embry-Riddle Aeronautical University. At the 13-year point (from entering school), this captain at Endeavor Air will be making $61,200 per year if everything goes exactly right.

Chapter Six
Upgrading to the Majors

In Chapter 5, I gave an example of our typical Embry-Riddle graduate and how his career will progress.

At some point, our pilot will want to leave the regionals and upgrade to the major airlines.

Generally, to be hired by the major airlines, a pilot must have captain experience at the regionals. At Endeavor Air, it is going to take six years to upgrade to captain and then another two years as captain before our pilot would be eligible to be hired by the major airlines such as American, Delta, Southwest or United.

It has now been 15 years since our pilot first walked into Embry-Riddle to begin his professional pilot career. He still has the student loan debt. He has been flying passengers for the regional airlines for eight years. At this point he is very experienced in flying. He is a very valuable asset to the company.

He starts sending out resumes to the major airlines. If he is hired, he will be hired as a first officer and have to work his way back up to a captain position. At some airlines this can take 15 to 20 years.

You would think that a pilot with eight years of airline flying experience would be making pretty good money. You would think that an airline would recognize how valuable he is. But you would be wrong. Our experienced, eight-year pilot will actually have to take a *pay cut* to go to work for the major airlines.

Here is the first-year pay our experienced, eight-year pilot would make if he upgraded to the major airlines:

American Airlines $36,480 per year

Delta Air Lines $61,608 per year

Southwest $53,352 per year

United Airlines $57,816 per year

US Airways $36,480 per year

In almost every other profession in the US, the more experience you have—the more you get paid.

For example, if you are an attorney and you switch law firms, you will usually make more at the next law firm than you did at the previous one. You will generally make more money as a 40-year-old experienced attorney than a fresh out of law school 25-year-old.

If you are a nurse, it works the same way. If you are a restaurant manager, it again works the same way. You almost always make more money when you switch companies because you have more valuable experience.

It does not work this way in the airline industry. If you switch airlines, you must start again at the bottom with first-year pay. In the industry this is referred to as "The Golden Handcuffs".

The Golden Handcuffs have kept pilot pay artificially low in the airline industry. Pilots are not able to "shop around" to find an airline that will pay them more for their experience.

The airlines have obviously used this system to their advantage. This system keeps employees working at below-market pay. It also keeps people working at an airline who would otherwise quit. Once you choose an airline for your career path, it is just about impossible to leave to go to another airline simply because you have to start all over again with pay and with seniority. Pilots have so much time and money invested in their careers that it becomes almost impossible to throw away everything that you have worked for and start all over again. The airlines have all promised that the longer you work at the airlines, the more money you will make.

Originally that sounded like a good idea. Come work for us. We will not pay you much the first year. But if you stick with us, then you will make really good money later.

When a pilot is hired, the airlines even provide a pay schedule promising the increases that a pilot will make each and every year. It all looks and sounds good. A pilot will top out in pay at the 12-year mark. If you are a captain at the 12-year mark, you will make pretty good money. The problem is that, in recent times, it has not been possible for airline pilots to get to the captain's position in 12 years.

Do you remember the USAir flight that landed on the Hudson River? The first officer on that flight was Jeff Skiles. He had flown more than 12,000 hours and had worked at USAir for more than 20 years. He still was not able to hold a captain's position without being on reserve. A 20 year plus USAir captain really does not want to be on reserve because the reserve flying schedules tend to be the worse ones and you cannot plan your schedules out in advance.

Reserve status for pilots usually goes to the new hires as the airlines integrate new employees and pilots into the system. A new pilot would be on reserve for a few months until they would be able to hold a line. It was never intended to be something that a long term employee would be subject to. However some airlines have subjected their long term pilots and flight attendants to being on reserve for over 10 years. If the airline has properly staffed their company with the people and planes then should not be a reason than any long term employee should be on reserve.

This is an important distinction. A 20 year first officer makes $51,480 less per year at USAir than a 20 year captain. A pilot who has been employed for 20 years at USAir and is flying an Airbus 319 as a first officer is paid $110,700 per year before taxes.

Every airline flying today broke those pay schedule promises except for Southwest Airlines.

If you notice the first-year pay chart from the major airlines, two of the airlines (American and US Airways) have much lower starting pay than the others.

US Airways pilots took a 40 percent pay cut during 2005 because the company was in financial difficulty. Those pilots have not recovered that 40 percent, let alone gotten their promised pay raises.

In the end those written promises did not mean anything to the pilots.

You would have thought that the US Airways pilots would have left in droves after getting a 40 percent pay cut. A few did. Most did not. It was because of those Golden Handcuffs. The pilots have too much invested, in their careers, to just walk away.

Chapter Seven
How Pilots Are Paid

You will hear airline executives claim to members of Congress or the news media that pilots are well paid. They will throw some numbers around that sound good. But first impressions can be deceiving especially when you are dealing with "airline math".

Pilots and flight attendants are paid by the flight hour. They are only paid when the doors are closed on the aircraft. This is an important distinction that is difficult for some to understand. The airlines really do not want you to know how this works.

If you take a flight on an airline there are a lot of processes and procedures that must happen. It is really a magical event as dozens of employees come together, each doing his or her part, to make sure your flight leaves on time and arrives safely at your destination.

Most airlines want passengers to show up one hour before the flight takes off. It is an option and not a requirement for the passengers.

However, for the pilots and flight attendants, it is not an option. The flight crew must arrive up to one hour before the aircraft is scheduled to take off. (Some airlines have a 45 minute report time)

The pilots will look over the flight plans as well as the current weather along the route. They will check with other departments at the airline to make sure fuel is properly ordered and the plane has no reported mechanical issues. They will brief the flight attendants about what to expect on the trip and whether there will be anything special that they need to know about. The first officer will do a walk around of the plane to make sure there are not any issues that would disrupt the flight. You might be surprised to know that the flight crew is not paid for any of this.

Did you know that before passengers are allowed to board an airliner that the required number of flight attendants must be on board? This is an FAA requirement. The reason for this is because if there is an emergency on the ground, the flight attendants must be able to evacuate the passengers.

When the plane begins to board passengers, the flight attendants are always there to greet you as you enter the aircraft. If you glance to your left you will often see the pilots in the cockpit going over their checklists, getting airport briefings and making sure the instruments are working and set up correctly. The flight crew is not getting paid for any of this.

After about 20 to 30 minutes, the passengers will all be on board and the plane will be readied for release from dispatch. The flight crew does not get paid for any of this.

You will then sometimes hear an announcement asking all passengers to take their seats and the door will finally be closed. The plane is ready to be pushed back from the gate. The parking brake on the plane is released. The time is noted. When the door is closed the flight crew starts getting paid.

When the plane lands and pulls into the gate, the pilots will set the parking brake and the door will be opened. Now the flight crew stops getting paid.

It will take about 20 minutes for all of the passengers to exit the plane after the aircraft has pulled into the gate. The flight crew is not paid for those 20 minutes.

If the plane is a quick turn, meaning that passengers will exit the plane and a new set of passengers will enter the plane, it will take a minimum of 45 minutes to turn the aircraft. The plane has to be fueled. The cabin has to be cleaned. The lavatories have to be serviced. Provisions have to be catered and accounted for by the flight attendants. Again, none of the flight crew is getting paid for this time because the parking brake is set.

If the crew has to change to another aircraft, they are not paid until the door is closed on the next aircraft. If the flight crew has to wait around the airport for several hours, they are not paid for that time.

A general rule of thumb is that when the flight crew is paid for one hour, they are actually on duty for three hours. So if a pilot is paid $25 an hour (that is what Delta's Endeavor pays their first year first officers) an hour you would actually divide that number by three to get the real hourly wage of $8.33 an hour. That is less than what fast food workers are paid and they do not have to spend $200,000 learning how to make hamburgers.

Pilots will fly about 75 hours per month. To fly those 75 hours, the airline will control 225 hours of the pilot's life, per month, including the time before and between flights. Some pilots will be on duty as many as 16 hours a day.

Keep in mind that if the average American works 40 hours per week, their employer controls about 160 hours of their time per month.

Chapter Eight
Pilots Are A Dime A Dozen

There is something about flying. Most pilots are passionate about it. It gets in your blood, and you cannot get rid of it no matter how hard you try.

That works to the detriment of pilot's pay. The airlines have known this for many decades.

At one time, just about every airline operated a flight training academy. Today, no airline currently operates a flight training school.

It used to not cost as much to learn to fly. The military trained thousands of pilots during World War II, the Korean war and the Vietnam war. Many of those pilots came out of the military and went to work for the airlines.

This provided the airlines with thousands of qualified and well trained pilots who were always available if an airline decided they needed to add pilots to their employee ranks.

There were so many pilots in the 1970s, 1980s, 1990s and 2000s that airlines had to lay many of them off and put them on furlough as the business climate changed.

In addition, two major airlines (Eastern Airlines and Pan American World Airways) ceased operations in the early 1990s.

This also increased the available amount of highly qualified pilots.

Some of these pilots were furloughed for six to 10 years. While the pilots were on furlough, they were not paid by the airlines, but they did maintain their seniority (original date of hire). This discouraged the pilots from going to work for a competing airline. If they went to work for a competitor, they would lose their seniority at their original airline.

This also discouraged experienced pilots from going to work with a startup airline unless they were former Eastern or Pan Am pilots who no longer had seniority because their airlines had shut down and gone out of business.

The airlines got used to having pilots available whenever they needed them. There was a saying that, "pilots are a dime a dozen". So airlines were quick to add routes and hire some more pilots. If it did not work out, they would cancel the routes and furlough the pilots.

Pilots were still on furlough at some of the major airlines until 2011. At that point, all of the furloughed pilots (who wanted to come back) had been recalled.

When the major airlines started hiring again in 2010, 2011, 2012 and 2013 they hired their pilots from the regional airlines. The regionals started having a difficult (but not impossible) time replacing the pilots who had been hired by the majors.

In 2012, most regional pilots were working overtime because just about all of the airlines were understaffed in the pilot department.

In 2010, Congress passed the Airline Safety and FAA Extension Act of 2010 which would take effect on Aug. 1, 2013.

The act required first officers for airlines to have a minimum of 1500 flight hours and an ATP certificate. *There is a reduction of the 1500 flight hour requirement to 1000 and 1200 hours under certain training programs and some approved four- year universities.*

Prior to this rule, first officers could be hired with 250 hours of flight experience. Although the rule did not take effect until Aug. 1, 2013, the effect of the rule actually started about a year earlier.

The reason for this is because no airline was going to hire any new pilot in 2012 that would not have the required 1500 hours by August 1, 2013.

The airlines had been given plenty of notice on this ATP rule going back as early as 2010. Most airlines thought that Congress and the FAA were bluffing and would back off from the rule. So, most airlines did not plan for it.

My experience has shown that most airlines do not plan very far into the future for anything. The multi-billion-dollar airline business is not run like normal businesses with one, three and five year strategic business plans. Everything seems to be run more in a crisis mode and things appear not to be planned for or accomplished until after the eleventh hour.

Jet Blue and Spirit Airlines are both major national airlines. Both airlines correctly read the tea leaves and realized they were going to need pilots in 2013. Jet Blue and Spirit Airlines started hiring pilots away from the regionals in 2012 and 2013.

There were also some work rule changes that came into effect on Jan. 2, 2014. The work rule changes required that pilots actually get eight hours of uninterrupted sleep each 24-hour period.

Prior to this time, pilots were getting as little as three hours of sleep each day. It took the crash of Flight 3407 to get the rule changed so that pilots could actually get eight hours of sleep before they get up and pilot a 500-mph jet aircraft carrying hundreds of passengers.

The passenger airlines fought this rule change tooth and nail for decades.

The cargo airlines (DHL, FedEx and UPS) also fought this rule and won. Unfortunately, at this time, their pilots still are not guaranteed eight hours of uninterrupted sleep.

On August 14, 2013 UPS Flight 1354 crashed on approach at Birmingham, Alabama. The plane was an Airbus A300. The NTSB ruled on September 9, 2014 that pilot fatigue contributed to the crash and loss of the crew.

In the end common sense and science prevailed for the airline pilots. If it were not for the Flight 3407 families, this rule would have never passed. They are to be thanked for their tireless persistence in this important area.

The work rule change created a demand for more pilots. Because pilots must actually get eight hours of uninterrupted sleep, they could no longer be forced to fly with just three to four hours of sleep. The flight schedules must be planned with the proper amount of rest prior to a flight. The time going from the airport to the hotel and back can no longer be counted as sleep time.

Just a note for clarification, the work rule requires that pilots get eight hours of uninterrupted sleep within a 24 hour period. It does not require eight hours of sleep before every flight. Most pilots fly several flights a day while on duty.

It is really no different than most other folks. You get eight hours of sleep, and then you get up and go to work. It works the same way with the pilots.

Every reasonable person would have to agree that pilots need eight hours of sleep. If you are a passenger riding in the back of the plane, you would not want pilots falling asleep in the cockpit, while the plane is flying on auto pilot, because they are fatigued.

The work rule changes were first discussed in 2009. The airlines fought them tooth and nail. They were delayed and delayed and did not take effect until Jan. 2, 2014. The airlines had plenty of notice and knew these work rules were coming. Some planned for the work rules and some did not.

The net effect of the work rules is that it takes more pilots to fly the airplanes. It is the same amount of flight hours divided among more pilots.

Prior to the work rule changes, it took about 12 pilots per aircraft to run an airline. After the work rule changes it takes about 15 pilots per aircraft to run an airline.

If an airline executive needs to know how many more pilots are needed, then he just needs to count the number of airplanes in their fleet and multiply it by three. This may be new material to some of those executives.

Chapter Nine
How The Aviation Industry Jumped The Shark

Transportation is not a new occupation or enterprise. Transportation has been going on for thousands of years as humans moved goods and themselves from one place to another.

It might have started with the caveman moving things from one cave to another. Later, wheels were invented. Then, ships were built that crossed the oceans from one land to another. Railroads were laid that allowed goods and people to cross the United States. Then, aviation came along about 100 years ago.

Aviation has evolved into often being the quickest, most efficient and fastest way to transport people and cargo across great distances.

Some cargo, such as fresh flowers and pineapples, could never be shipped to arrive fresh and useful if it were not transported via aircraft. Smaller cargo, such as mail, or lightweight objects can be flown across the country overnight. There is currently no faster way to move something over a long distance than an aircraft.

Aircraft travel the world every day with cargo that keeps factories running.

As the population of the US and the world grows, the demand for air travel also grows. The more people there are, the more need for air travel. It is a pretty simple concept.

Back in 1991, Eastern Airlines was one of the big four airlines. When it shut down on Jan. 18, 1991, Eastern had 304 aircraft in its fleet.

Later that year, Pan Am, one of the world's largest airlines at the time, shut down on Dec. 4th. Pan Am had 226 aircraft in its fleet.

In 1991, these airlines were two of the largest in the world. There would not ever again be another pure shutdown of an American-based airline of the size of these airlines.

One other notable airline shutdown was on May 13, 1982 when Braniff International Airways shut down. At the time of the shutdown, Braniff had a fleet of 82 aircraft.

In 2014, American Airlines has 1,546 aircraft in their fleet counting the American mainline, American express, USAir mainline and USAir express aircraft.

In 2014, Delta Air Lines has 895 mainline and express jets in its fleet.

In 2014, United Airlines has 711 mainline jets in its fleet.

If we just compare fleet size, you can see Delta is more than 10 times the size Braniff was when it went out of business. Delta is more than three times the size Pan Am was when it shut down. Delta is almost three times the size of Eastern Airlines when it shut down. Airlines have gotten much bigger. There are great efficiencies for airlines as they get bigger. They also become better choices and values for the customers who patronize those airlines.

Air travel has grown as the population has grown, and it will continue to do so.

Aviation has had its ups and downs during the past few decades. When the economy is growing, the airlines have typically done well. When the economy is contracting, the airlines have dismal results. All major airlines flying today have been through bankruptcy at least one time (except for Southwest).

There are five big airlines today: American, Delta, Southwest, United and US Airways which has now merged with American but is still flying as US Airways for the next 18 to 24 months.

All five of these airlines were around prior to airline route deregulation. American, Delta and United were large airlines before deregulation. All of these legacy carriers are now many times larger than they were before deregulation. They have the same name today as they did prior to deregulation.

Southwest was very small. USAir was a regional airline principally serving the Northeast part of the US from a Pittsburgh base. It was named Allegheny Airlines prior to deregulation. Allegheny Airlines changed its name to USAir in 1979 as deregulation took effect.

Southwest is a very important part of aviation history in the US. It grew to become the largest domestic air carrier in the US, but has now become eclipsed by the larger airlines merging together.

Southwest started flying in 1971 after a four year legal fight. At that time, Southwest only flew within the state of Texas. Three airlines in business at that time, (Braniff, Continental and Trans-Texas) started legal action and did everything in their power to crush Southwest and keep it from flying. They were not successful and Southwest pushed and pushed and worked around all of the obstacles that the other airlines had put in its path. Southwest changed aviation history by thinking outside the box.

As a start-up, Southwest's costs were lower. They were more efficient, and they could sell tickets for less than the other airlines. That was an advantage at that time.

In the 1980s, 1990s and 2000s, if the other airlines matched Southwest's lower ticket costs, the other airlines would lose money on every competing ticket they sold, while Southwest made money on every ticket it sold.

As far as I know, Southwest never intended to sell any tickets at a loss. That was not its business plan. If it could not make money on a route, it would cancel the route and move the aircraft to where it could make money.

In the early 1990s, Southwest had a cost per air passenger mile of about 7 cents. Competing airlines had a cost per mile of

11 to 14 cents. In simple terms Southwest's costs were 30 to 50 percent less than all of the other airlines.

Southwest would enjoy this cost advantage through the mid 2000's. During this time, Southwest would grow six times its 1990 size to become the largest domestic airline in the US.

Passengers benefitted in the form of lower ticket prices. The legacy carriers just could not compete and they all struggled from 2001 through 2005 as Southwest was growing and actually making money while all of the other major airlines were unprofitable and in danger of failing.

All of the legacy carriers were forced into bankruptcy to survive. While in bankruptcy, the legacy carriers were able to restructure their airlines to operate at a cost lower than Southwest. This was a game changer, and the game is not over yet.

The result today, is that Southwest has higher costs than the legacy carriers and, in many instances, cannot sell tickets as low as the legacy carriers can.

There are two main reasons for this. The main reason is fuel cost. Today, fuel costs are the airlines biggest expense representing up to 35 percent of the gross revenue of the airlines.

Also, Southwest now has a more mature work force. Those employees are now some of the highest paid in the aviation industry. At one time, they were some of the lowest paid.

Chapter Ten
Airline Executives in Denial

I do not know how some airline executives come up with this stuff. Instead of trying to actually solve the problem of the pilot shortage, which is caused by poverty pilot wages, they continue to push back and attempt to continue these substandard wages that qualify pilots for food stamps.

Airline executives have a unique way of adding numbers together. I call it "airline math". Airline math really does not add up very well, but these executives keep doing it over and over again.

On April 30, 2014, Bryan Bedford, chairman, president and CEO of Republic Airways testified before the House Committee on Transportation and Infrastructure Subcommittee on Aviation.

According to Bryan, Republic Airways is a large regional carrier with 6300 employees and more than 2,200 pilots.

Bryan is attempting to persuade Congress to relax the 1,500 rule which he is claiming to be the cause of Republic not being able to hire enough qualified pilots (It is not).

Bryan went on to attack the GAO Aviation Workforce Report which was released on Feb. 28, 2104.

The GAO report concluded there were currently enough available pilots, but, in effect, they were not able (or willing) to work for poverty wages.

Bryan then testified that the median annual wage for US airline pilots was $114,200 in May 2012.

That was really convenient for him to provide this number. That way we can compare the median annual wage to the annual wage that Bryan pays his pilots at Republic.

What Bryan failed to let the committee know was that none of the 2,200 pilots at his large regional airline makes anywhere near $114,200.

In fact, no pilot at any regional airline makes anywhere near $114,200 a year. Furthermore, there are many pilots at the major airlines who do not make $114,200 a year. Bryan's airline math just doesn't add up.

The *top pay* for a first officer at Bryan's Republic Airways is $33,300 a year. It does not matter if you have worked at Republic for four years or for 20 years, Republic will only pay a first officer a maximum of $33,300 a year.

For years one through three, the Republic pay is even worse. Year one is $20,700 a year. Year two is $27,900 a year. Year three is $32,400 a year.

For year one, this equals a gross pay of $1725 per month. From that gross pay, the pilot will have to deduct his health insurance cost of $749 per month. By the time taxes and union dues are deducted the take home pay is less than $700 a month at Republic Airways. That qualifies a pilot for food stamps. It is not the pay that a professional should earn that has spent over $200,000 getting his training. It is not even close to the $114,200 that Mr. Bedford testified to Congress about.

By the way, Republic does not pay pilots if the flight is cancelled for mechanical, scheduling or weather issues. So, if the pilot shows up at the airport and there is something wrong with the plane and it cannot be flown, the pilots and flight attendants do not get paid. It does not matter if they have commuted from half way across the country and had to stay in a motel overnight in order to report for duty one hour before scheduled takeoff. If the plane does not fly the flight crew does not get paid.

It will take a new hire pilot seven years to upgrade to captain at Republic. The new hire pilot is going to be stuck at $33,300 a year from years four to seven.

What Bryan is not telling you is that if a new hire is flying 70 passengers in the back of one of Republic's aircraft, on a one hour flight, then each passenger is paying 33 cents of the ticket price to the first officer pilot. Compare that to what a cab driver makes when he has passengers in the back seat!

This airline executive cannot figure out why Republic is having trouble hiring new pilots while he intentionally misleads Congress.

Mr. Bedford, I stand willing to give you and any other airline executive a thorough lesson in economics and the cost of living in the United States. The US taxpayer should not have to subsidize your pilots by having to provide food stamps to them.

Mr. Bedford is also Chairman of the Regional Airline Association's Pilot Task Force. You would have to think that anyone on that task force is drinking the same Kool-Aid as Mr. Bedford.

Obviously Mr. Bedford is not the only airline executive who feels that pilots should make poverty wages.

The management of American Eagle (now Envoy) is just as misguided. They probably have been drinking the same Kool-Aid that Mr. Bedford partakes. The former president of American Eagle, Daniel P. Garton, now is on the board of directors at Republic. He was unanimously elected to this position by the Republic board of directors, effective Jan. 3, 2014.

The current rate of pay for a new hire at Envoy is $22,464 per year. At year two the pay increases to $29,376. At year three the pay increases to $31,968. There is a seven year upgrade to captain at Envoy so a new hire is going to be making $35,424 at year seven.

But what is even more bizarre at Envoy is that as I write this book in 2014, airline management is trying to get the pilots to take another *pay cut*. The pilots already took a pay cut to help keep the company out of bankruptcy. The company got the pay cut and filed bankruptcy anyway. Now American has emerged from bankruptcy and is the largest airline in the world.

It is expected that American Airlines will make more than $3 billion in profit this year.

That strong financial position has not discouraged American from continuing to pay their new hire pilot poverty wages.

American threatened to outsource the flying to Republic or another bottom feeder regional airline if the current American Envoy pilots would not agree to a pay cut.

The Envoy pilots did vote down the poverty wage agreement, and American is attempting to outsource the flying to Republic. The problem is that Republic cannot find pilots to work for poverty wages and already has parked several dozen planes in 2014 because they do not have pilots to fly them.

I've got a lot of faith in Doug Parker, who is now the CEO at American Airlines. I would hope that Doug will step up and do the right thing and realize how valuable his pilots are.

The only thing that can limit the growth of American Airlines (or any other airline) is the lack of qualified pilots.

An airline can train most airline employees in a short period of time to do the job properly and serve customers. The only airline employees who cannot be trained in a short period of time are the pilots and the mechanics.

An airline can buy as many airplanes as their checkbook will allow. As long as airplanes are available, the only thing stopping an airline from getting additional planes is money. Airlines frequently pre-order aircraft and they also sell and trade those slots as business conditions change.

I know of a certain airline that had contracted with Boeing for some aircraft. The airline did not need those aircraft when they were ready to be delivered because business conditions had changed.

The airline simply took delivery of the aircraft from Boeing and flew them to Miami where they sold them to another airline that needed the planes right away. The original airline actually made a profit when it sold the new planes. This same scenario was repeated several times by this airline. So, planes are always available one way or another. Airlines sell and lease planes to each other.

However, it takes five to eight years to train a pilot to airline proficiency. Without pilots, an airplane cannot fly, and all of those other employees who support that aircraft will not have a job.

At some point, pilots pay is going to have to be increased to a reasonable standard of living for a trained professional. The first airline executive who does this will get the pilots and set the standard for a proper and reasonable living wage.

The airlines are certainly in a financial position today to pay professional pilots a professional wage.

Chapter Eleven
Mainline, We Have A Problem

2014 started off a bit different in the airline industry. The new work rules were finally in place that allowed the pilots to actually get eight hours of sleep each night.

These rules probably affected the regional airlines more than the majors. The regionals were more likely to have pilots work longer for less because of the way they overnight planes at the outstations.

For example, prior to the new rules, when a crew brought a plane in at 11:45 p.m., that same crew took the plane back out at 6:00 a.m. It was impossible for pilots to get eight hours of sleep with that schedule.

The net effect was that each airline needed to add three additional pilots for each of the aircraft they have in their fleet. The majors actually did a pretty good job of adding pilots. They simply hired them from the regionals.

The problem comes when the regionals try to replace those pilots by offering poverty wages. Some of these regional airlines are in a real pickle. They have bid their contracts too low and not taken into account the increased cost of pilots.

Of course there are four wholly owned regional airlines. Delta owns Endeavor Air. American owns Envoy, PSA and Piedmont.

The wholly owned airlines can fix this with the stroke of a keyboard. It's an internal decision that affects only their airline. It's just going to take money.

So far, none of the wholly owned airlines has made any effort to cure this poverty wage problem at their regional airlines. In fact, they have done just the opposite and asked for concessions that they do not need. They did this because they thought they could get away with it. After all, they have been getting away with it for a couple of decades.

Express Jet is another large regional airline that is owned by SkyWest Airlines. Express Jet flies for American Eagle, Delta and United.

On Jan. 14, 2014, ExpressJet pilots voted on a new tentative agreement. The poverty wage tentative agreement was rejected by 83 percent of the pilots voting. 91 percent of the eligible pilots participated in the voting. This was the first shot fired over the bow in the regional airline industry. Obviously there are a lot of unhappy and broke pilots at ExpressJet.

This ExpressJet vote was a game changer. It was the first time in recent history that pilots voted down a contract in the regional airline sector.

Just four months earlier in September 2013, pilots at PSA Airlines (a wholly owned subsidiary of US Airways) had agreed to a new contract. Some 61 percent of the pilots had voted for it. The contact, was not a good one for the pilots. In fact the American Eagle pilots had voted against the same contract just a few months earlier. But the PSA pilots succumbed to the airline management threats and promises and ended up voting in a new concessionary contract. Now the PSA pilots will not get raises. Their pay is capped at the four year level and they have to increase their medical benefit contributions from 27 to 35 percent. That will probably be the last one of this type of contract ratified by a pilot group for a long while.

Feb. 10, 2014 marked the first time that airlines publicly acknowledged that they had to cancel flights because of a lack of pilots.

It was the first time that an airline acknowledged it had to permanently remove planes from the fleet because there simply are not enough pilots to fly those planes.

2014 would be a game changer year for the pilots and the regional airlines.

Those regional airlines that choose to adapt to the current economic conditions will survive. Those that do not make the needed economic changes to attract and hire qualified pilots will go out of business. At least two regional airlines will go out of business this year.

Bryan Bedford from Republic Airlines was the first to make the announcement that some of us in the industry had known and predicted for several years.

ExpressJet and Great Lakes made the same announcement that day.

Flights were being cancelled and planes were being removed from the fleet because these three airlines cannot hire qualified pilots to fly their aircraft.

It has gotten so bad that Great Lakes Airlines has removed 10 seats from their Beech 1900's (formally 19 seat aircraft). They did this because a technicality in the FAA rules allows an aircraft with nine seats or less to be exempt from the first officer ATP requirements if the plane is legal to fly with a single pilot and is flown under a part 135 Air Taxi Service certificate.

So technically, Great Lakes can fly their Beech 1900's with 10 seats removed with just one pilot and be legal with the FAA. What stops them from doing it are the insurance companies. Thank goodness insurance companies require two pilots up front if you have paying passengers in the back.

Since the second pilot is not required by the FAA (under Part 135) in this instance, Great Lakes can hire a 250 hour commercial rated pilot to fly in the right seat on the aircraft if it has nine or less seats. About 80 percent of Great Lakes business is Essential Air Service routes. They do have codeshare agreements with Delta, Frontier and United.

Great Lakes Airlines will pay a first year pilot a gross wage of $1200 a month and it will not pay the new pilot during his first three months of required training at the airline.

Regional flight cancellations have been going on since 2011 when Pinnacle Airlines started cancelling hundreds of flights per month because of a lack of flight crews. This would lead to Pinnacle Airlines bleeding red ink and having to file bankruptcy.

In 2014, things are much different for the airlines. American Eagle pilots were in a nasty battle with American management which wanted to cut the low wages in effect since 2004 to even lower wages in 2014.

American management had been threatening to take the flights that American Eagle pilots had been flying and transferring those flights to Republic Airways and shutting down American Eagle if the pilots did not agree to the concessions.

There was absolutely no reason for American management to ask for these concessions. American Airlines is predicted to earn more than $3 billion in profits in 2014. That is the most American Airlines has ever made in the history of the airline.

With the Feb. 10, 2014 announcement from Republic Airways, the pilots knew that American management could not transfer those flights to Republic because Republic was already forced to park planes because of the lack of pilots. ExpressJet could not accept any more American Eagle flights because it was cancelling flights with United because of a lack of pilots.

In February 2014, the Master Executive Council (MEC) at the ALPA American Eagle union rejected the proposed agreement without sending it to the members for a vote. The company cried foul and tried to divide a wedge between the pilots and the union.

In March, the union did agree to send the agreement to the pilots for a vote, and 70 percent of the pilots at American Eagle voted against the new poverty wage concessionary contract. It turned out the MEC was correct.

Silver Airways is based in Fort Lauderdale Florida. It is a regional feeder for United. Silver also has some essential air service routes. In March 2014, 84 percent of the Silver Airways pilots voted against their new proposed poverty wage contract.

Silver is now offering a $12,000 signing bonus in an attempt to recruit new pilots. Right now, they have six pilots per aircraft at the company and they have had to remove all of the remaining Beech 1900's that were in its fleet. It needs 15 pilots per aircraft. Silver will probably need to start paying a retention bonus to keep the pilots they still have.

In April 2014, Republic Airways sent a new proposed four-year poverty wage contract to their pilots for a vote. The contract was rejected by 85 percent of the pilots who voted. It appears there are not many happy pilots at Republic Airways.

Chapter Twelve
The Sky Is Not Looking Good Out West

SkyWest, Inc. currently operates two of the 17 regional airlines in the United States.

SkyWest owns SkyWest Airlines and ExpressJet Airlines. ExpressJet was originally a subsidiary of Continental Airlines which was spun off as an independent airline in 2002 (Remember mainline airlines do not like to own regionals).

In 2010 SkyWest owned Atlantic Southeast Airlines (ASA) which it had purchased from Delta Airlines in September 2005.

In August 2010, SkyWest announced that it had made an agreement to acquire ExpressJet Airlines, Inc. by merging it with Atlantic Southeast Airlines. The deal was completed on November 12, 2010.

SkyWest in one form or another operates flights for almost all of the major airlines including Alaska, American, Delta, United and USAir.

In 2013, SkyWest flew 60.6 million passengers on their aircraft. The total revenue passenger miles flown in 2013 was 31.8 billion.

This is a combination of two super regional airlines that you probably have never heard of because the sides of the aircraft say Delta or American or United or USAir depending on the city in which the aircraft are based.

During the first quarter of 2014, the mainline airlines offered SkyWest additional flying opportunities. The pilot shortage was starting to cause problems and the airlines continued to dangle carrots at the regional partners.

ExpressJet went on a very active pilot recruiting effort in order to gain this additional business from their unnamed mainline partners which were believed to be American, Delta and United. They put a lot of time and effort into recruiting every qualified pilot they could find.

There were a couple of problems with this effort.

The first problem was that the current ExpressJet pilots did not have a new contract. The contract that was presented to the current working ExpressJet pilots was rejected by 83 percent of the pilots voting.

The second problem was that ExpressJet was attempting to hire the new pilots at $20,700 per year.

The recruiting effort failed. So there would be no new business and there would be issues with keeping the current aircraft flying.

Unexpectedly in May 2014, SkyWest replaced their president, executive vice president and chief operating officer.

This is not a good sign. One senior executive leaving is enough to raise eyebrows. Replacing three senior executives at the same time is a disaster. It often is a signal of things to come.

On August 6, 2014, SkyWest announced some pretty dismal second quarter results. While their mainline partners were making billions of dollars in profits, SkyWest was losing millions of dollars during the same time period.

There is a combination of things happening here. There is a shortage of pilots causing flights not to be completed. When flights are not completed passengers are stranded and SkyWest does not get paid.

Because of the shortage of pilots, some flights are not completed on time. That means SkyWest does not get paid as much. There are incentive bonuses that are not paid when flights are late or are not completed.

SkyWest (in their race to the bottom) underbid their flying contracts with their mainline partners. The result was that SkyWest was losing money on many flights that they actually were completing.

On August 8, 2014, SkyWest made an announcement that was buried in their financial results. By the end of 2015 SkyWest was removing 157 regional, 50 seat jets from their fleet. This is the equivalent of 1,758,400 revenue passenger seats per month.

The 157 regional, 50 seat jets are going to be replaced by 40 regional, 75 seat jets. This is the equivalent of 672,000 revenue passenger seats per month.

If you do the math, you will see that SkyWest will have a net loss of 1,086,400 revenue passenger seats per month. That turns out to be a loss of 36,213 revenue passenger seats per day.

Keep in mind that most of the routes SkyWest has been flying are popular routes that have over an 80 percent load factor. So the passengers are currently in those seats. When these seats are removed from the air transport system, those passengers are going to have their flights cancelled.

Those 36,213 revenue passenger seats per day represent gross annual ticket revenue of $1.89 billion. This is an important number.

It's a number that the airline executives do not seem to understand.

You see, SkyWest could solve their pilot shortage by paying the pilots a professional wage. It would take an additional $90 million to pay the pilots to fly those parked aircraft. That is the equivalent of five cents to gross one dollar. The airline executives do not understand this concept at this time. So they will give up the dollar and strand 36,213 passengers per day because they will not spend the extra nickel.

You must keep in mind that SkyWest is just one of the 17 regional airlines that are part of this process.

As revenue passenger seats are removed from the commercial air transport system this will cause three disruptions.

1. The remaining planes will be more crowded.

2. There will be more passengers that want to fly than there will be available seats. This will create a higher demand for airline seats.

3. As the demand increases for airline seats the cost of the tickets will increase.

In the beginning, the airlines will remove planes from the smaller cities in order to keep their aircraft flying. Those cities that have only regional airline service are the most at risk.

The cities with the lowest passenger counts may see their service totally discontinued. Passengers in those cities will need to drive 100 or more miles to a larger city in order to be able to board an airliner.

Other medium size regional airline cities may find their frequency of flights reduced. If your city currently has four flights a day, that number could be reduced to two flights per day.

All because the airlines do not want to pay the pilots a professional living wage for their service.

Chapter Thirteen
Where Is All Of This Going?

Reality and economics came together in 2014. Even though beginning pilots have always been eager to work a short time for poverty wages, it is just no longer possible.

Any young person who happens to have $250,000 laying around in an education fund or trust account is not going to "invest" that money into a profession that pays $22,000 the first year and $35,000 for the next eight years. The young person could keep the money safely invested, stay at home, do nothing and make more money investing that $250,000 than what is currently being offered to pilots.

In the past, airlines were able to hire pilots anytime they needed them. There were always pilots around.

Today there are enough licensed commercial pilots to fill all pilot openings at the airlines. According to the GAO there are currently more than 60,000 ATP rated pilots that are not working for the US airlines. Because the airlines need about 4,000 new pilots a year, the pool of 60,000 pilots should be enough to fill those 4,000 annual pilot openings for the next few years.

Most of these commercial pilots have moved on to other careers because the pilot pay is so low. You cannot expect a person to leave a $100,000-a-year job to go to work as a pilot for $22,000 a year. The numbers simply will not work.

The airline industry suddenly experienced a pilot shortage in 2014. Part of the reason for this shortage is a lack of planning by the airlines. The other reasons are passenger growth and low pilot pay.

The airlines asked the Government Accountability Office to do a study to determine whether there is a pilot shortage.

The GAO quickly conducted a study of the current and future availability of airline pilot and released its findings, as a 61 page report, in February 2014.

The GAO study found that both pilot employment and earnings have decreased since 2000. There are not many industries in which employees are making less in 2014 than they were in 2000. In fact, I do not know of another industry in which employees are paid less in 2014 than they were in 2000 for doing the same job.

The study concluded that the median weekly earnings for pilots had decreased by 0.8 percent per year from 2000 through 2012.

The annual rate of employment growth for pilots has actually decreased by 12 percent from 2000 to 2012.

So while airlines were contracting, and laying off pilots, the pay for the pilots who remained was cut. These cuts were agreed to by the pilots to keep the airlines in business during the difficult business period after the Sep. 11, 2001 terrorist attacks.

Now that the industry has recovered and is actually growing, pilots are having a difficult, if not impossible, time regaining the wages they gave up and have not gotten a pay raise. Of course, costs for housing, gasoline, fuel and just about everything else have gone up during the past 14 years.

The airlines now find themselves in a growth mode. Increased passenger traffic means airlines can put more aircraft in their fleets if they can hire the pilots to fly the aircraft.

The current pilot shortage can be fixed simply by paying pilots a proper wage for the job they are doing. There are enough licensed ATP pilots available for the right price.

Looking forward, there will be an acute pilot shortage in the future. This is because there are not enough students currently in the training process to fill those future positions.

At one time, all of the airlines had training academies for pilots. Those academies were first put in place because there was a lack of pilots. At that time, the fastest and most cost-effective way to obtain pilots was for the airlines to train them.

Every airline academy was eventually shut down as airlines were able to hire pilots who had been trained elsewhere. This transferred the initial pilot training costs away from the airlines.

My belief is that the airlines will need to re-establish flight academies to guarantee they will have enough pilots in the future. These training academies will be a hybrid-type facility that will focus on professional airline training from the beginning. There should be an apprenticeship program at the US airlines. Today, that does not exist.

There is a reason that an apprenticeship program at the airlines really is a good and necessary idea.

I am going to expose one of the secrets that the airlines do not want you to know.

Let us look at a typical new hire today at the airlines. He is going to be hired with at least 1,500 hours and an ATP rating. He is going to be hired to fly a passenger jet at 500 miles per hour.

This new hire pilot will be hired by the airlines, and he will be put through three months of training. During this time, he will be training on a number of things, including the aircraft that he will be flying as a first officer. The airlines have simulators at their training facilities that mimic the cockpits of actual aircraft. However, these simulators are not airplanes, and they do not fly. This is an important distinction.

The pilot will come out of the three-month training program and he will be put on the line with a check pilot for a 30-day period. A check pilot is generally an experienced pilot that works for the airline and has the ability to teach and transfer information in a positive fashion. During this time, the check pilot is furnishing additional training and evaluating the performance of the new hire.

But what the airlines do not want you to know is that the check pilot is teaching the new hire while there are passengers in the back of the plane on scheduled flights.

Most people do not know that the first time a new first officer actually gets to fly a real jet is when there are passengers in the back.

Obviously a new hire has to start somewhere and it is difficult and expensive (if not impossible) to get experience in an actual jet.

I would like to see part of the apprenticeship program include a ride along, with some assigned duties, on the jump seat for a period of time.

This would allow the new hire to observe how things work and flow with two experienced pilots at the controls. Currently, FAA rules do not allow pilots to do this, but the FAA Part 121 rules require aircraft dispatchers to ride along, on the jump seat, at least five hours a year.

Chapter Fourteen
Why Airline Executives Do The Things That They Do

The airline industry is a unique industry in the United States. Although there are hundreds of thousands of people employed in the industry, there are very few executives.

I need to bring up an example from another business to help demonstrate what I believe is going on in the airline business.

I have been involved in several other unique industries and businesses during my lifetime.

I was involved in the miniature golf industry and, at one time, worked for the two largest mini-golf operators in the country.

That industry was so unique that when the founder of the Putt-Putt mini golf chain (Don S. Clayton) died, there was not anyone who could step in and fill his shoes to run the largest mini-golf chain in the world. As a result the Putt-Putt franchise system which once had more than 300 locations dwindled to less than 50 locations.

At its peak, the Putt-Putt system employed thousands of people. Yet, out of those thousands of people, not one would rise to the top and successfully steer the Putt-Putt business into the future on a positive growth rate.

I believe the reason for this is because in order to lead such an organization, you must be able to see the big picture. You have to understand each and every part of your business.

Among other things, you have to fully understand what makes your customers patronize your company. You have to understand how to motivate your employees to make sure your customers are well taken care of.

Sometimes, it is the little things that make a big difference.

Piedmont Airlines was absorbed into USAir in 1989. Piedmont was famous for always giving their customers a full can of soda. Twenty-five years later, folks still talk about Piedmont always giving their customers a full can of soda instead of just a glassful. You see, that little thing made a big difference that people still remember.

I know the Putt-Putt business would still flourish if Don Clayton were still in charge. Unfortunately, the types of Don Clayton are very rare, and they do not come around much.

I believe it is the same thing with airline executives. Unless they see and understand the big picture, they simply repeat what past airline executives have done—right or wrong. They do not really understand how all of the pieces of this industry fit together.

I stated earlier that unions are a necessary evil in the airline industry. This is because there are so many employees at the airlines. With an executive team of just a few who have to manage tens of thousands of employees, it is an impossible task without written contracts that are agreed to by the unions. Without unions, the working conditions would be stretched to unsafe levels.

On the other side of the table, the unions also have a problem. They have to represent thousands of employees with just a few leaders.

This creates a condition that renders the unions not as effective as they could be.

As a result, you end up with a relationship between the unions and airlines that can be described as strange at best and totally screwed up at worst. When the big picture is not seen by everyone, things can get very fuzzy.

I am convinced that some airline executives and union leaders do not actually read and understand the financial statements their accounting departments produce. I believe if they actually took the time to understand the financial statements, they would not keep reducing pilot wages.

So, let me try to put some numbers together that are easy to understand. Keep in mind that a dollar is a dollar and it still contains 100 cents.

US airlines sell tickets that cost dollars. That allows us to break down a dollar, that an airline takes in, to help demonstrate how all of this works.

Let us just pretend that Delta Air Lines sells a ticket for $100. Out of that $100, here is where Delta's expenses are distributed that you might find of interest:

Fuel cost $25 (largest cost)
Wages for all employees $21 (second largest cost)
Cost of plane $2
Cost of maintenance of plane $5

There are some other expenses as well, such as insurance, catering, depreciation, commissions, landing fees, etc. But I believe that if you understand the four expenses that I have listed, you will know more than most airline executives.

Those four expenses represent about 53 percent of Delta Airlines gross revenue.

The item that one might think is the biggest cost (the aircraft) is actually the least expensive cost on the list. This is the reason that airlines can buy or lease planes. It is a small expense compared to all of their other expenses.

If you look at the cost of maintenance you will see that it is around 5 percent of Delta's budget. Aircraft have to be serviced under strict FAA rules and schedules. The older the fleet, the more an airline will spend on maintenance.

Sometimes it is more cost-effective to purchase new planes than continue to fly older aircraft. New aircraft are under warranty and do not require as much maintenance. New aircraft are also more fuel efficient.

Let us look at the ways that costs can be cut. Let us say an airline executive wants to cut the cost of planes. Maybe he will buy Airbus instead of Boeing because Airbus aircraft are less expensive. Maybe he will buy the stripped down version instead of the super deluxe version.

If the cost of the aircraft is 2 percent of the revenue of the airline, what is the maximum amount an airline executive can save if he shops around for an aircraft? If the airline executive could save 10 percent in this category the savings would be one fifth of a cent per dollar. If the airline executive could save 33 percent in this category, then the savings would be less than 1 cent per dollar of airline revenue.

If you think about it, there isn't a big reward for an airline executive by cutting expenses in one of the lower cost categories. The most he can save is a fraction of a penny out of each dollar.

Now let us look at the biggest expense which is fuel. That is 25 cents out of each dollar. If the airline can save 10 percent in the fuel category, that would be 2.5 cents out of each revenue dollar. If the airline can save 33 percent on fuel then that would be 8 cents out of each revenue dollar. That could really add up. Just a note, Delta's fuel cost is lower than most other airlines for a number of reasons including the ownership of a refinery.

So a prudent airline executive would always look to cut his biggest expense since the reward is so much greater than trying to cut a smaller expense.

Now we get to wages. Wages, salaries and benefits, at Delta, are 25 cents out of each dollar that the airline collects. That is not an unusual number for many businesses in the United States.

If you are an airline executive, at first glance you might think that the pilots are getting 25 percent of the ticket revenue. That would not be true. That 25 percent includes the cost of all employees at the airline including the airline executives!

So let's break this down a bit in real airline numbers. I am going to use Delta Air Lines as an example. Its percentages will not be much different than the other airlines.

According to publicly available data, Delta has about 80,000 employees today. Delta has 722 aircraft in its mainline fleet. That works out to 110 employees per aircraft. Delta has 11,723 pilots. That works out to 16 pilots per aircraft. To put it another way, 14 percent of the employees at Delta are pilots and 86 percent of the employees at Delta are not pilots.

In 2013, pilot pay (including wages, taxes and benefits) at Delta represented 5.1 percent of the airline's gross revenue. This is an important number to know. The reason this number is important is because airline executives have constantly attacked pilot pay.

If airline executives actually understood that 5.1 percent number, they would not spend time and effort attacking that number. The reason is because there just is not much to be saved in this expense category.

The only way that any potential savings would be possible is if the airline were overstaffed with pilots. Because there is a pilot shortage and because the FAA requires at least two pilots per aircraft, it would be difficult to establish that the airlines have too many pilots in 2014.

In addition, the pilot position is the only position at the airline that cannot be quickly filled. It takes many years to make a pilot. Today it will be seven to nine years before a pilot will have the experience to fly for the airlines.

Airline HR departments can take every other position at the airline (including airline executives) and fill that position with an intelligent person, (who has never done an airline job before) with just a few months of training. They cannot do this with pilots. In 2014 they are finding this out the hard way.

To put it another way, if an airline executive could actually save 10 percent on pilot pay (which they cannot), that would account for one half of one percent of the airline's gross revenue. It's not even close to a full percent. That is hardly any benefit to keeping the airline in business.

At many airlines today (excluding Delta) fuel cost represents 35 percent of the airline's gross revenue. This expense is the biggest threat to an airline. This fuel expense number is unsustainable for the long term and it has continued to increase.

On the other hand, if an airline executive could save 10 percent of the biggest expense, which is fuel, then that number would account for 3.5 percent of an airline's gross revenue. And that would be a worthwhile savings.

Part of managing a business is knowing what expenses can be adjusted as well as when to adjust them.

Paying the pilots poverty wages is not part of good business planning or management.

Chapter Fifteen

UPGRADE TIMES AND PAY

As I write this book in 2014, the upgrade time from first officer to captain at Delta is 14 years. So a pilot hired at Delta today will not be a captain at Delta until 2028.

Of all of the majors, Delta currently has the fastest upgrade time at 14 years.

American Airlines current upgrade time is 21 years. United is 18 years. USAir is 26 years.

This is important, because first officers make 40 percent less than captains. If the upgrade times in the future are the same as in the past, pilot pay will continue to be depressed if left at current levels.

For example, let us take our 2014 student just entering Embry-Riddle Aeronautical University. If everything goes well, here is what his future looks like under a best case scenario:

2018 -- He graduates with 250 hours of flight time and his multi-engine instrument commercial pilot certificate. He will have obtained his CFI rating which allows him to teach others to fly. He will have amassed $207,000 in debt at current tuition levels. His monthly payments on the student loan debt are $1199 per month until 2048.

2019 -- He works for a flight school, teaching students to fly. He is paid (on commission) about $10 per flight hour for the hours he is flying and he is instructing. When he is not flying or instructing, he does not get paid even if he is "on duty" at the flight school. He is lucky to take home $250 a week.

2020 -- He continues working at the flight school, building time towards the 1,500 hours that he needs to obtain an ATP rating. He is still making $250 a week.

2021 -- He now has his 1,500 hours and he is eligible to obtain his ATP rating. That rating is expected to cost $20,000 in 2021. Once he has that rating, he will be eligible to be hired by one of the regional airlines. If he goes to Republic Airlines, he will be paid $1725 a month. He will be at Republic for the next nine years until 2030.

2022 -- He is now flying as a first officer for Republic Airlines. He gets a pay raise to $2,325 a month. This is the largest pay raise that he has ever had and will be the last big one for six or seven years.

2023 -- He continues flying as a first officer. He gets a pay raise to $2,700 a month.

2024 -- He continues flying as a first officer. He gets a pay raise to $2,775 a month. This will be his last raise for the next four years. It has now been 10 years since our student first walked into Embry-Riddle Aeronautical University, and this highly trained college graduate is now being paid $33,300 a year to fly 50 to 90 passengers in a jet aircraft.

2025 -- He continues flying as a first officer and he makes $33,000 a year. He has been with the airline five years. If he leaves to go to another airline, he will start all over again at $1725 a month or $20,700 a year.

2026 -– He continues flying as a first officer for $33,000 a year.

2027 -- He continues flying as a first officer for $33,000 a year. However, if everything goes right he may be able to upgrade to captain soon.

2028 -- 14 years after entering Embry-Riddle our pilot has now upgraded to captain. He gets a pay raise. This will be the biggest pay raise in his career thus far. He now is paid $5,625 a month or $67,500 a year.

2029 -- He continues flying as a captain gaining the PIC time that he needs to get hired by the majors. He now makes $5,775 a month or $69,300 a year.

2030 -- It has now been 16 years from the time our student entered school. This is his third year as captain. He now makes $6,150 a month or $73,800 a year. He is looking to move to the majors. He sends out his resume. He gets hired by Delta.

2031 -- It has now been 17 years and our student has reached his goal of flying for the majors. He is now a first officer for Delta. He had to take a pay cut to come to Delta.

He expects to be able to upgrade to captain in 2045. That will be 31 years since he started at Embry Riddle. His pay this year is $5,100 a month or $61,200 a year. He had to take a $12,600 a year pay cut to come to Delta.

2032 -- Our pilot gets a big pay raise this year. He now makes $7,050 a month or $84,600 a year. This is the most money he has ever made.

2033 -- Our pilot gets another big pay raise. This is the last big one for a while. He now makes $8,250 a month or $99,000 a year.

2034 -- He continues flying as a first officer. He now makes $8,400 a month or $100,800 a year. This is the first time he has made $100,000 a year as a pilot. It has been 20 years since he started at Embry-Riddle and 16 years since he graduated. He still has not been able to extinguish his student loan debt.

2035-2044 -- He continues flying as a first officer waiting to upgrade to captain.

2045 -- It is 31 years since our pilot began his studies at Embry Riddle. He is now a captain and he will receive a pay raise. He now makes $150,000 a year at Delta.

It took 31 years to get there.

Chapter Sixteen
There Is Only One Solution

I don't know that you will find anyone that would truly believe that a trained professional should earn anything *close* to poverty wages for any reason whatsoever.

There are four components that have caused poverty wages to be the norm for an airline pilot.

1. The Railway Labor Act
2. The airlines
3. The unions
4. The pilots

Only one of the above components actually has the ability to solve the poverty wage problem. Let us briefly examine these four components.

RAILWAY LABOR ACT

The Railway Labor Act is a federal law that governs labor relations in the railroad and airline industries. It was first passed in 1926 and amended in 1934 and 1936.

The law was first put into effect to prevent a shutdown of the railroads by the employees. It was later amended to include the airline industry.

In effect, the RLA prevents airline employees from going on strike without first going through a long mediation process followed by a 30 day cooling off period. The mediation process can last for years.

Even when airline employee contracts have expired, because of the RLA, pilots are not permitted to stop working or permitted to go on strike.

What ends up happening is that contracts can be expired for five years and an airline has no incentive to negotiate a new contract. There is no real penalty to the airline for letting a contract expire.

What has been happening is that airlines just drag out the contract negotiations as long as they possibly can. Their reasoning has been it is cheaper to pay the employees under the old contact than the new one.

I can think of two examples where this happened. In 2000, the USAir flight attendants contract had been expired for about three years. The flight attendants fly the same schedules as the pilots at USAir. However the flight attendants are represented by a different union.

No matter how hard the flight attendants tried, they could not get the company to give them a new contract that provided for adequate pay and working conditions. USAir management had dragged the negotiations out for five years. Finally the flight attendants called for the 30 day cooling off period.

USAir executives did not settle this during the 30 day cooling off period. The result was that the flight attendants called for a strike on the eve of the cooling off period. Midnight came and went and thousands of USAir flight attendants gathered near the airports with picket signs.

At 3:45 a.m. the next morning, the company agreed to a new contract. The flight attendants did not go on strike, but without a new contract that morning, USAir would have not been able to fly much of their fleet. In all reality, the flight attendants should never have had to go to this extreme just to get a contract. The issue should have been settled years earlier.

The most recent incident that I can remember is the Spirit Airlines pilot strike of 2010.

On June 12, 2010 at 5:01 a.m. Spirit pilots went on strike after going through three years of negotiations and a 30 day cooling off period like the USAir flight attendants had gone through in 2000. It should have never have come to this. The strike lasted five days and Spirit Airlines lost millions of dollars every day that their planes did not fly.

Spirit management was actually asking for a pay cut during the three year negotiation process. It was pure nonsense out of the "old school" airline management playbook.

As a result of the strike, today Spirit pilots are well paid, customers get extremely low fares and the airline is the most profitable airline (percentage wise) of any of the US domestic airlines.

The amount of money the pilots are paid is such a small percentage of the airline's gross revenue, that it does not even move the needle.

THE AIRLINES

The airlines are companies that exist to move cargo or passengers from Point A to Point B.

The airlines are managed by executives. Like any business, airlines cannot exist unless they make money. That is a given.

Like any large business, because so much money is at stake and runs through airline hands, airline executives relentlessly are always looking for ways to cut costs.

Airlines will set a budget for each department and each expense category.

At one time in the US, pilots were paid very well. However pilot pay has degraded over the past years for a variety of reasons. The GAO study concluded that pilot pay has been on a steady decline since 2000 and pilots in 2014 are paid less than pilots were paid in 2000.

Since pilots were once paid well, airline executives still believe that pilot pay should be a category that costs can be cut. In fact there is not one major airline executive that currently believes otherwise. If they did believe otherwise, they would not insist that pilots work for poverty wages in 2014.

Evidence shows that airline executives do not know how to properly budget their expenses and costs.

Airline executives need to start budgeting the pilot expense category to reflect adequate, true and proper costs for a paid professional that is trained to safely transport thousands of passengers each and every month. There is no reason that a trained professional should ever have to work for poverty wages.

THE UNIONS

This one can be a can of worms. The pilots complain about the unions. The airlines complain about the unions. The unions are necessary in the airline business because of the size of the airlines and the number of employees that are employed and based all over the country.

Unions collect union dues from the pilots. Pilots often don't think they are getting good value for their dues. That may or may not be true depending on the time, place and airline. The airlines know this and sometimes will attempt to exploit a relationship. I'm not going to get into all of that here. The book is about poverty wages—not labor union relationships!

The airlines complain about the unions because unions can cost them money. So there is relationship conflict issue right from the start. However the airlines must accommodate the unions and for the most part they do just that. But the airlines are experts at manipulating the unions when they see a need to do so.

So the union is caught in the middle between the individual pilots, the airline and the Railway Labor Act. This results in the unions having to do a balancing act in order to get anything accomplished.

When I was in flight school, one of the pilots from the airline came in to give us a presentation. At that time, he told us not to get involved with the union because we were not going to be at the regional airline for very long. He explained that the company frowns upon those that get involved with the unions. That may or may not be true, but if it were true, I don't believe any airline executive would admit it.

There is no question that the unions have dropped the ball on the pilot pay. This has allowed the airlines to keep the pilot pay artificially low. But we cannot just blame the unions for this.

THE PILOTS

There are a number of airlines. Some airlines have hundreds of pilots. Some airlines have thousands of pilots. One thing is for sure. You are not going to get all of the pilots to agree on everything. There are just too many of them.

While in flight school, I had a mentor pilot. This was a pilot that was currently flying for an airline. We would communicate just about every day about things. I would know his schedule. He would know where I was in my training.

We talked about many things during and after training. One of the things he told me was that pilots are like sheep. They don't like to step up. They can be herded as a group (like sheep) and just do as they are told by the airline. They will pretty much go along with what the company wants.

There is some truth to this. Many pilots are like sheep. The airlines know this. For example, the airlines know what to say to scare those pilots when they need to have a new contract ratified.

When American Eagle recently presented a poverty wage contract to the pilots, management told the pilots that if they did not accept the contract, management was going to shut the airline down, send the planes to one of the other bottom feeder regional airlines and the pilots would be out of a job.

Many pilots believed management and voted for the substandard contract anyway. However most pilots looked at the contract and realized they were already broke and just could not handle any more pay cuts. The contract was voted down.

So far in 2014, three other regional airlines have had their proposed contracts voted down by the pilots. There is a reason these contracts are being turned down in addition to the poverty wages.

In the past, airline pilots have not been at the regional airlines for very long. When a poverty wage contract was presented to the current pilot flying group, those pilots knew they were not going to be at the regional airline for much longer. Within another 12 to 18 months they would have moved on to one of the majors and the contract they were voting on would not really affect them once they were gone. They could collect a fast signing bonus and let future new hires deal with the poverty wages.

Today, pilots are spending nine or more years at the regionals. So those poverty wage contracts are really affecting all of the pilots. That is one of the reasons they are now being voted down.

THE ONE SOLUTION

Out of the four components, only one has the ability to offer a true solution in 2014.

The Railway Labor Act is a law. Nothing in the RLA can solve the pilot poverty wage problem. If the RLA were abolished, that would still not solve the problem in 2014.

The union is a catalyst between the pilots and the airlines. Nothing the union can do will solve the pilot poverty wage problem in 2014.

The pilots can only agree or disagree with what is offered to them. Nothing the pilots can do will solve the poverty wage problem in 2014.

That leaves the airlines. The airlines are the only component that has the ability to solve the pilot poverty wage problem in 2014.

The airlines must set up their budgets to properly reflect the proper and true cost of a professional pilot in 2014.

This is not a hard thing to do. I have listed a detailed timeline of a pilot career in Chapter 15. It is a very simple matter to determine what the proper professional airline pilot wage is at three years out of school, five years out of school, ten years out of school, etc.

If a pilot is going to spend at least $200,000 in addition to six to eight years training to become an airline pilot, a reasonable person would have to believe that at some reasonable timeline, that pilot should be making at least $100,000 a year.

Delta and American can immediately solve the poverty wage problem with their wholly owned regional airline subsidiaries. It can be done with keystrokes.

Delta owns Endeavor Airlines. They can solve this issue tomorrow.

American Airlines owns regional airlines, Envoy, Piedmont and PSA. American Airlines can solve this issue tomorrow.

Once these two airlines solve the poverty wage program within their regional airlines, then the remaining regional airlines will be able to solve their issues as well.

There really is no other solution. Airlines need to acknowledge the problem and go ahead and solve the problem. The longer they wait—the worse it gets.

In the end, economics have caught up with pilot wages in 2014. If the airlines do not solve this poverty wage issue (that should have never existed in the first place) then they will be forced to park planes and lose the revenue that those planes produce. That is exactly what is happening in 2014. Remember the pilots are paid pennies out of each airline ticket sold. The money is there to solve this problem.

In addition, flights to many of the smaller cities in the US are going to be cancelled as the remaining pilots will be moved to routes between larger cities.

Currently there are not enough pilots in the training pipeline to staff US aircraft fleets in the future. It takes six to eight years to train a pilot to airline proficiency. The pilots entering school today will not be ready to come online until 2021.

www.ingramcontent.com/pod-product-compliance
Lightning Source LLC
Chambersburg PA
CBHW072059290426
44110CB00014B/1746